ADVANCE PRAISE FOR

MANTLE MATCH

★ ★ ★ ★ ★

MANTLE MATCH NOT ONLY OPENED MY EYES TO THE DEPTHS OF MY SPIRITUAL CALLING BUT ALSO GUIDED ME ON A PROFOUND JOURNEY TOWARD ABUNDANCE IN EVERY FACET OF LIFE. A TRANSFORMATIVE READ THAT UNVEILS THE SACRED LAYERS OF EXISTENCE, LEAVING THE READER INSPIRED AND EMPOWERED TO EMBRACE THEIR UNIQUE PATH WITH PURPOSE AND FULFILLMENT."

ALLISON BETHEA-BROWN

★ ★ ★ ★ ★

MANTLE MATCH IS A WORKMANSHIP SPECIFICALLY DESIGNED BY THE HAND OF GOD. THE DOWNLOADS IN THIS BOOK, PENNED BY AUTHOR, KISHA PURNELL, HAVE AN ASTOUNDING MESSAGE OF FORTIFICATION THAT WILL IGNITE AND TOUCH THE HEART OF THE READER TO MOVE INTO THE DIRECTION OF THEIR PURPOSE. A VERY ANTICIPATORY ANOINTED READ.

CARMELA E. HEAD

★ ★ ★ ★ ★

MANTLE MATCH GIVES VERY REAL AND PRACTICAL WISDOM AND INSTRUCTIONS TO BOTH MEN AND WOMEN WHO ARE SERIOUS ABOUT BUILDING GODLY HEALTHY MARRIAGES AFTER FIRST EXAMINING AND PREPARING SELF.

REV. ANGEL OJ THOMPSON, PH.D.

WELCOME TO THE

M

MANTLE MATCH JOURNEY

KISHA R. PURNELL

MANTLE MATCH ™

PREPARING, PROCESSING, HEALING & WHOLENESS WHILE WAITING ON THE PROMISE

THIS IS A WRITTEN WORK BY
Kisha R. Purnell
PUBLISHED BY The LEGNA Agency LLC

The Mantle Match

Published in the United States of America by
Kisha R. Purnell
An imprint of The LEGNA Agency LLC

www.KRMinistries.net
www.MantleMatch.com

Library of Congress Cataloguing-In-Publication Number
2023923980

ISBN 978-0-9833592-2-7

First Edition Printing
Printed in the United States of America
December 2023

Kisha R. Purnell
8208 Hudson Forest Drive
Charlotte, NC 28269
www. MantleMatch.com
www.krministries.net

TABLE OF CONTENTS

(F) FOREWORD 9

(I) INTRODUCTION 11

(1.) PREPAREDNESS 15

(2.) PROCESS 26

(3.) LIFE LESSONS 36

(4.) OVERCOMING REJECTION 47
& DISTRACTIONS

(5.) I'M NOT PERFECT 57

(6.) YOU ARE ENOUGH 65

(7.) THE WAIT 72

(8.) I AM WHOLE 83

(9.) DEAR FUTURE HUSBAND 97

(A) ABOUT THE AUTHOR 108

(J) JOURNAL PAGES 109

MANTLE MATCH™

THIS BOOK IS DEDICATED TO
MY FUTURE HUSBAND.

I LOVE YOU DEARLY AND
THANK YOU FOR CHOOSING
ME.
YOUR LOVING WIFE~ KISHA

ALSO, TO MY AMAZING
CHILDREN KAYLYN, JAKYIA
& DEVARI.

MY MOTHER GLADYS
PURNELL, GRANDMOTHER
MARY McKINNON,
AND FAMILY.

THANK YOU FOR YOUR
PRAYERS AND SUPPORT!
FAMILY IS IMPORTANT!

#ITSGENERATIONAL

ALL THINGS ARE
WORKING TOGETHER
FOR MY GOOD.

MANTLE
MATCH

FOREWORD

In the sacred tapestry of our lives, there exists a divine thread woven intricately by the hands of destiny. Kisha Purnell, in her profound odyssey titled "Mantle Match," unravels the very fabric of her soul, exposing the raw beauty of her spiritual pilgrimage.

As we embark on this transformative journey, the title itself, "Mantle Match," beckons us to explore the celestial choreography of God's plan for love. It is not merely a search for a life partner but an exploration into the sacred grounds of a God ordained union a cosmic dance orchestrated by the Creator Himself.

Kisha's words echo the universal heartbeat of those who yearn for a connection beyond the mundane, seeking a match not only in the earthly realm but in the celestial corridors where destinies are forged. "Mantle Match" becomes a profound revelation, unveiling the layers of healing and wholeness required for a divine assignment, a marriage preordained in the heavenly scrolls.

This book transcends the boundaries of personal narrative; it is a sacred testimony of resilience, faith, and surrender. Through the tapestry of Kisha's life, we witness the divine alchemy that transpires when one's heart is aligned with the grand design of the Creator. Each chapter unfolds a sacred script, inviting readers to reflect on their own paths, as they too navigate the sacred grounds of preparation.

In the sacred silence of introspection, readers will find echoes of their own longing and discovery. Kisha's revelations serve as a guiding lantern, illuminating the path toward a deeper understanding of self, a profound connection with the divine, and the unfolding of a purpose beyond the tangible.

As you turn the pages of "Mantle Match," may you feel the resonance of your own spiritual journey, the gentle nudging of a divine hand, and the whisper of destiny calling you to prepare for your Kingdom Assignment. Kisha Purnell's narrative is not just a memoir but a sacred invitation to join in the dance of celestial unions, where healing begets wholeness, and where love is not just found but divinely matched.

Dr. Torrey Phillips
The Faith Factory Firm
Fort Lauderdale, Florida

INTRODUCTION

Mantle Match| When I started hearing this from the Holy Spirit, I immediately started researching. What is a Mantle Match? Mantle refers to a cloak or covering. It also describes the transfer of power. The mantle represented a man's gift, the call of God, and the purpose for which God had called him. A match is a person or thing able to contend with another as an equal in quality or strength. There were several questions before God regarding "Mantle Match" and how this applies to me and my life.

As a little girl, I always dreamt of the storybook romance and marriage. I saw myself being married and in a loving, long union with four children. I desired to have two girls and two boys. But guess what? Life did not turn out as I had imagined. I went through a divorce like so many others have. I only had two biological children of my own. This was a turning point in my life. I found myself at a crossroads. That's when I embarked on this journey of rediscovering who I was and what I now wanted in life.

I had no desire to get married again. I asked myself over and over again, "What have I done to be in this place"? Why me? As I was reflecting one day, I received confirmation that I would love again, but that "You cannot get married again for the sake of getting married." were God's exact words to me. I knew this time it would be a "Kingdom Connection."

What is a "Kingdom Connection"? A Kingdom Connection is a divine connection orchestrated by God for His (Kingdom) purpose. It is a covenant that I believe God designs so that both of our lives will benefit the world, and destroy the works of the enemy.

This term is often thrown around casually, but I knew this was serious. How would this Kingdom Connection be established? Faced with considerable uncertainty I knew I needed insight from Holy Spirit that would shed light on this and what it meant for my life personally. What I was about to enter into, I had no clue. Little did I know, this would become an unfolding and revealing of me, to me.

Simultaneously filled with excitement, nervousness and a fear of the unknown, one thing was for sure God was yet speaking. This would be a "God thing" that would become a high level threat to the forces of darkness. This would be more than a relationship, it would be a covenant sanctioned by God, designated and designed to build each other up in our Kingdom assignments. This was all very deep to me, and I knew I needed wisdom as I journeyed in this endeavor. This is how God began the process in me that eventually led me to give life and language to the journey for others in the form of this book.

This book is for anyone who has found themselves at a crossroads in life and is seeking The Lord for their God given identity and mandate in life and love.

Whether relationally or spiritually my prayer for every reader is that while you are in "the wait" these principles given to me by Holy Spirit will add greater insight and value to you in every area as you are being healed and made whole.

"There are some things that you need to do while you "wait," is what I heard Holy Spirit say to me. Healing and forgiveness were essential to name a few.

As I unpack these principles and share my personal story of what God was unveiling along the way. I hope that this book gives encouragement and offers hope along with practical application that will be helpful so that everyone may embrace and enjoy their time of singleness and prepare for the "Mantle Match".

HE MAKES ALL THINGS
BEAUTIFUL IN TIME

01
PREPAREDNESS

Still, I hear God. In the Spring of 2022, I received prophetic instructions. "Prepare Now!", to be concise Holy Spirit said, "If you wait until it comes to pass to get ready it will be too late. Make the adjustments NOW!" These words put fire under my feet and a sense of urgency that provoked me to move. I knew what this word meant for me in more than one area of my life, but in the application part, I was unsure where and how to begin. The Lord was prompting me to get ready to begin again. As I began seeking The Lord, He began to download insight and principles to me and how they would benefit me in my future marriage. This was a time of much prayer and meditation for me and the genesis of my process.

The first principle given was **preparedness**. As stated, I never thought I would be in this place called divorce, ever. However, I quickly learned, that there is indeed life after divorce. No matter how old you are or how long you have been waiting, I want to reassure you that God can use it all. Nothing will be wasted. What does it mean to prepare? In this context, it means to make it ready for use or consideration. It's the make ready for use or consideration for me, that spoke volumes to my heart. Make ready for use or consideration this was not just speaking to my social status but my spirit. God was making me ready for His use and His consideration! This principle needs to be addressed first. This "season" may look different for each of us. To be ready for purpose and destiny to collide, preparing now is key to the advancement of the next. Preparedness was more than just the first principle; it was strategically placed because it starts with a mindset. It's so much greater than just a task or checklist of things to do then the right person will find you. It's about a journey that God wants to take you and me on as we heal and embrace what is. So, whether you are newly single or have been for a while, being single does not mean that you are alone or even lonely. Being single is not bad. Let me start by saying that. It's all in

God's timing, the due season the set time. There is a plan for your life, and it shall manifest at the appointed time. Live in the moment and enjoy every day.

Singleness should be a time of rediscovery and of loving oneself. A time to build or rebuild. What does that look like? For one, this could mean a need to repair credit depending on one's circumstances. For another, it could mean developing routines that will foster love within one's family, returning to finish the degree, or even attending therapy. The list is endless. Whatever you do, don't waste this time! That's why it is especially important to prepare in your singleness so that you are ready when the promise shows up.

You can't get ready. You must be ready when the opportunity presents itself. For me as a divorcee, I had to relearn various things. At first, I was very bitter about it all. These were my questions: "Why Me God". Why didn't you stop this? What did I do in life so badly that caused me to have to deal with this? Then I started to look at it from another perspective and I took my time of singleness to start preparing and allowing Holy

Spirit to restore me and my life. My mindset and focus began to shift. Let me say this, things don't have to be perfect before God allows that "someone" to come but the season should be stewarded well. I started implementing and executing the strategies that Holy Spirit was releasing to me. I became very intentional about ministry assignments, fostering mental wellness and putting myself first and my physical health. I wanted the best version of me to be present for me. My time preparing was and has been a long journey. There was much healing that was needed. I didn't realize just how much until I was deep in it.

Regardless of how you arrived at this social status and how long or not you have been here, you are single. Singles of all ages have dealt with life challenges and for most of us life has brought pain and even trauma. I wanted to do all that I could to ensure that I was emotionally whole and mentally well before engaging in a long-term meaningful relationship again. I knew that I needed to bring the best of myself to the table without so much baggage from prior relationships and a failed

marriage. There were tough realities that I had to face. Primarily, I needed to find myself again. Along the way I had forgotten who I was. Serving in the ministry for years, working in corporate America, and owning my own business, not to mention being a wife and mother, had caused me to lose sight of who I was and what was important to me. See, I was a "fixer". Oftentimes I put others' needs before mine and I never took the time for myself and all that I was giving out was not being given back to me.

There is an adage that says, "You can't give what you don't have" and for years I poured and loved from a place of deficiency not even aware this was happening. By doing this for so long, it became my norm and because of this, I had to learn to find my way, love myself and rediscover the woman that I no longer knew outside of my world of chaos. So, in my preparedness time, I had to forgive others and most importantly myself so that I would move past the memory of all I had endured. Some that were self-inflicted. In highlighting this point, I want to emphasize its importance so that it is not forsaken. Forgiveness is essential in the healing process. I have heard that "life is so short" when in reality life is so unpredictable. Here today gone today not tomorrow. Life has taught me that things can change suddenly and with this knowledge, I choose to live every day as if it's my last.

Yes, it was hard starting over, and I didn't want to, but guess what? Life happened and now I needed God to help me to put the pieces back together again, even dreading the fact that I would have to, but God was with me and led me the entire way. I found my strength in Him. *"And he said unto me, My grace is sufficient for thee: for my strength is made perfect in weakness. Most gladly therefore will I rather glory in my infirmities, that the power of Christ may rest upon me". 2 Corinthians 12:9*

There were countless sleepless nights and times of not knowing but my faith carried me through it all. I could not do it in my own strength. As I stated earlier "Preparing oneself starts with a mindset" A prepared mindset is essential to having a "Kingdom Connection." What is a Kingdom Connection? It is paired with one of the same likenesses and

mindset that is ordained and designed by God for his plan and will. It is God-ordained. I knew that I could not do things the way I had previously. This time, I wanted to do it God's way. God guided me through this time. One major takeaway was that self-care was okay and very much needed.

This time should be spent pouring back into oneself, becoming centered as you hear from Holy Spirit. Being true to yourself will help you to know where to begin. I was very practical in my approach. As God gave the instructions, I journaled them and executed them according to His plan. Everyone has their journey and path to embark upon.

It's all about the journey and not the arrival to the destination, as I was once told by a mentor friend of mine. I did not want to rush this principle. Each one brought healing and deliverance. I was starting to feel like myself again. There was newness and a refreshing deep within. An inner healing and cleansing taking place and I was ready to continue on my quest.

When I think of preparing, I think of new parents who are expecting a new baby. They buy all the essential items and create this beautiful nursery so that they have everything prepared; and what's needed at the arrival of their new addition. The room is filled with love and there has been attention to every detail that could be imagined. As a new parent, it's about convenience and not so much the cost. If it's needed, then it's needed!

This principle let me know that no matter what it cost for me to be prepared it would cause me to have to make some sacrifices. Not all of them would be easy. When God showed me this, I could imagine a beautiful nursery in soft colors waiting for a new bundle of joy to appear. God speaks. Stay in a place of expectancy you never know if the bundle could arrive early. Through preparedness, this gave me a sense of hope and joy. I was expecting something from God! I knew that he would deliver and right on time!

Now that I had prepared, the next principle was process. I simply wanted to forego this principle altogether. Theodore

Roosevelt says it best "Nothing worth having comes easy." If you think that it does, then you are mistaken. The things that we strive the hardest for will often bring great pain and much adversity but will eventually yield a great reward.

01

PREPAREDNESS

LET'S DO THE WORK!

In your journal write down the things that you are feeling. This gives a documentary of your thoughts as you go through this journey.

Commit to the Lord whatever you do, and he will establish your plans. Proverbs 16:3 NIV

MANTLE MATCH

TODAY I GIVE MYSELF
PERMISSION TO
EXPLORE THE NEXT.

MANTLE
MATCH

02
PROCESS

Principle Two Process Whew. This step was equally hard. Nothing or no one has ever been presented without process. The scripture text of Joseph and how he was sold into slavery by his own brothers because they disliked him, unbeknownst to them, it was God's plan for Joseph to precede them so that he would be able to save his family and generation in a time of a great famine. What a long road Joseph had before which had been not just about him, but it was for others. Life can take us to places we never thought we would ever go, but God's plans lead us to where we are supposed to be. In between the prophecy and promise is the process. What is Process? One definition is that it is a series of actions or steps taken to achieve a particular end or goal.

From a spiritual meaning, it's a time when God takes us through inner development to try and prove us for the assignment that we are called to. Never forsake the processing of anything. This is invaluable! So, preparation and process are intertwined. An example of the process is a collection of action items to be decided on. As you prepare you now need to create an action plan for getting it all done and a reasonable timeline. For me, I went with the rhythm of Holy Spirit. Again, I did not want to have to repeat any steps so I decided early on that I would be patient in my discovery and extend grace to myself that I often give to others. In my season of process, this was both spiritual and natural for me. God was birthing something through me and in me, I had to allow myself to go through the process. Don't get stuck "THERE." Preparedness and Process required me to relinquish my control and surrender myself to God's careful hand. I was reminded that I cannot just prepare, arrive, and then perform. So, while I was preparing and being prepared, I was also being processed. It took significant prayer for me. There were things I thought I knew that I didn't know and things I had forgotten. However, God brought them back to my remembrance. Preparing and

Processing are two different things, however, quite different principles that are yet correlated. This principle is about going deep into what steps you need to take to achieve the desired result. So, God said to me "I need to develop you in your new assignments and ministry". My reply was "Yes Lord." My mindset was shifting, and I began setting my affections on things above and not on the world. My perspective had changed. I did not have all the details and didn't know what that was going to look like, but God did. *Jeremiah 29:11* says, *"For I know the plans I have for you," declares The Lord, plans to prosper you, and not harm you, plans to give you hope and a future."* God did not send any of us here without a plan. The plan God had for my life was predestined and predetermined before the very beginning of time. So, then we all must go through our process. Just as Joseph did. You may very well be the "deliverer" for your family just as he was.

When we hear the word Process, mostly, it's related to pain and yes it can be painful, but the process is simply allowing God to take you through development to become who you were designed to be from the very start. Forsake not the season of refining, healing, and purging. Just allow God to bring you out tried, tested, and proven by Him, not man. God will get the glory.

There were feelings of being stuck and stagnant, not able to move forward but refusing to go back. I had come too far to turn, look, or even think back. I was in too deep. Everyone's process will look different, and it should. My prayer became "Lord strengthen me in the wait and strengthen what remains". Asking Him to rebuild me where I had been torn down and remove the memories of hurt from it all. Still not knowing what was next, I learned to trust God even more daily. I would awaken to a freedom in Him that I have never known. "Lord, I Trust you" became my mantra, and to this day it still is. God was requiring me to trust Him on a higher level. As I was evolving into this woman that He desired me to be, looking within myself, and in doing so, I discovered certain things that were deeply rooted that had to be uprooted and destroyed. This was a very painful time for me, yet I persevered with resiliency. *"Do not grieve, for the joy of The Lord is your strength" Nehemiah 8:10* I began to look within and reflect. I uncovered many things that were hidden within myself that I did not like and there were many truths I had to deal with. This gave me hope and so then it was easy to embrace the NOW and move forward in the new. A time of inner healing and letting go of the past opened the window. My direct instructions given were "Forward Movement". It was time to let the past be just that and not only accept but embrace the new things.

Am I invisible? Does anyone see my pain? Did anyone know what I was going through and had gone through? I was having a pit experience and God had me hidden. I did not know that then. God had me in this place so that my process would cultivate perseverance from within which revealed to me who I was and more importantly whose I was the apple of my Father's eye and how I was loved. At one time I had forgotten this. My eyes were opening. There was enlightenment and awareness that was being formed from within and I was beginning to see myself as Christ saw me. Preparedness and Process took a while and I'm still on my journey. I am still on the potter's wheel. God is saying to us today don't worry so much about the process but to remember the promise. A promise is still a promise! I just love God and how He keeps His word that was spoken over my life and yours.

It's already promised. *Haggai 2:19 NLT.* *"I am giving you a promise now while the seed is still in the barn. You have not yet harvested your grain, and your grapevines, fig trees, pomegranates, and olive trees have not yet produced their crops. But from this day onward I will bless you."*

From this day onward I will bless you! What a magnificent reassurance of a sovereign God. I take courage that our God is not going to wait until the work is done before He will bless us. Our Father rejoices at the start. Yes, before the harvest even comes, before we see the full manifestation of the work, before that thing is even produced; there is a promise to us, and it starts at the foundation of it.

I remember God was taking me through a purging and a time of release. He had told me to get rid of some things that I didn't want to let go of. He told to me take it down to the foundation. Seeing the strength of a thing is only as strong as the foundation on which it stands or sits. In choosing to take it to the core of the thing ensures that it would start strong and fortified! Reinforced by God. Strengthened by God, that's what He's doing, not only in my life but yours as well. He's building back up what was torn down. He says from today onward I will bless you. The start of your healing journey has begun.

THE COVENANT PROMISE PRAYER

Father, I thank you that you are faithful and that you keep your word for the promises of God are Yes, and Amen. It is so and so it is. Your love has never failed me and from day to day I see your love and your mercy renewed every day. My faith is unwavering because I know your nature and character. You are an amazing Father. The rainbow after the flood is still evident today which is a reminder to me that you change not. I thank you for the promise that is to come. One that you will bless me from this day onward. As I walk in obedience to your will, your way, and your plans for my life. I will stay in a place of expectation of what is to come. I rejoice in knowing that you hear me, you see me, and you know me by name. You have summoned me, and my answer is yes Lord. From then to now and forevermore your word is established and settled in heaven. Thank you for the Covenant Promise that is over my life between you and me. I renew my commitment and my life with you. I trust you, Lord! I trust you, Lord! Just as you did before you will do it again. I'm grateful. Amen

02

PROCESS
LET'S DO THE WORK!

Create an action list of things that you need to complete/work on. Be as detailed or not as you want (sort of a checklist) in your journal.
Examples:
Create a budget.
Work out 2-3 days a week.

And I am sure of this, that he who began a good work in you will bring it to completion at the day of Jesus Christ. Philippians 1:6

MANTLE MATCH

NOT HAVING ALL THE DETAILS- I EMBRACE THE UNKNOWN.

MANTLE MATCH

03
LIFE LESSONS

It was in my quiet time as I was reflecting, that I wondered," Where was God?" Being in what I called one of the toughest seasons of my life, I felt like I could not breathe and that I was holding my breath. Dealing with all that life had thrown at me and so many other challenges all at the same time, to say it was overwhelming would be an understatement, yet there was such a peace that I could not explain. A peace that surpassed all understanding! There were thoughts that this could never happen to me. I found myself in a very unfamiliar place and it was a place of loneliness and isolation. I was in a place of despair and uncertainty. I prayed and I cried out to God. Through the fear and frustration, I realized I was in my wilderness place and that God had me right where I needed to be on my face seeking Him for direction and instructions.

The voice of everyone around me was silenced and all I kept hearing was what I thought was so small but was profound "Be Still and Know." In a place of uncertainty, I then started thinking about my life and all the things that I had been through that got me to this place. I began to accept this time of isolation and consecration before The Lord and, in doing so, He began unfolding His plans for my life. This caused me to hold myself accountable for numerous things which I had overcome. I identified myself as an overcomer. There were various lessons that I identified with the help of a professional. As I said earlier, I was a "fixer." A Fixer is attracted to people they can fix. They will try to help that person, give them attention, check in with them, always be there for them, give them emotional support, and try to fix their problems by giving advice, like a free and unlicensed therapist. I was trying to play God! Okay, that was too much for me to do and so then I found myself attracted to this personality type in relationships and it was overwhelming and emotionally draining for me since I was not getting the same in return.

There was a need to feel valued and wanted so this satisfied that desire and gave me a sense of belonging. I did not know this was what I was doing, but as I became aware I knew this had to stop so I became intentional about breaking free of the patterns in my life that caused me to keep going around and around in circles and cycles. I allowed God to continue to do the necessary work needed in my life with a newfound love for myself, my well-being began on all levels. Self-love is an amazing thing. There were times I thought myself unworthy of God's love, but as I came into an awareness of His unwavering love for me, I was able to love myself. He still loved me despite me. This helped me to realize that He loved me unconditionally. Not based on what I knew, what I did or didn't do but just because I was me. Life had given me many lessons and I had to learn a lot of things the hard way. Not because I was hardheaded or not willing to listen but because I did it my way. I remember hearing God speak to me regarding navigating and He said, "I want to take you another way". For a long time, I failed to consult God as I should have. Knowing His word that was spoken to me many times before *"Trust in The Lord with all thine heart, and lean not unto thine own understanding. In all thy ways acknowledge him, and he shall direct thy paths.* **Proverbs 3:5-6**

Not acknowledging The Lord as I should caused me much pain and, I would move at times before I received confirmation from God. So, this kept me in cycles of self-sabotage because I would allow my inner voice to keep beating me up with my past decisions. "Why did you do this or that?" I could go on and on until one day God said to me "STOP it I have forgiven you". Self-sabotage is a terrible thing to do to oneself. I didn't know it then, but I would do this to tear down or discredit myself, what God was speaking, or anything before I was rejected by man. It was a safety net for me. Let me do this to myself before others do it to me. God says no more. I come that you may have life and have it more abundantly. I was my own worst enemy. This came so naturally to think that others were thinking or viewing me in the most negative light as if they could see all that was right in my life. Get out of your head. The inner voice that speaks to us, if they are contrary to what The Lord says about us, do not receive this as the truth. That's why the Bible instructs us to cast it down.

*"Casting down imaginations, and every high thing that exalteth itself against the knowledge of God, and bringing into captivity every thought to the obedience of Christ;" **2 Corinthians 10:5***

Principle three, LET IT GO! I was still holding on to all that I had gone through and my poor choices. This was why I could not move forward. There were many things that I had learned, the first one was life happens. It's not so much as to what has been dealt to us but rather how we deal with the hand that we are given. Letting go and letting God be God would require me to relinquish my control, and that was exactly what He was requiring of me. One summer night when I was very young and trusting, I found myself in a very awkward situation as a young woman. I trusted a guy to give me a ride home after work and

that was a mistake. I learned that everything that meets the eye is not always what it is.

Thankfully I was able to get home safely and with minimal harm, but I knew it was because of the Grace of God. He has been with me and has provided divine protection. I did what I knew to do, I prayed "Lord help me out of this situation". Even after this, I was still engaged in communication with this young man knowing I should have cut ties but the fixer in me trying to "fix him" which was beyond my control. This caused me to endure things that I should not have. I love how kind God is and He directs us even when are not aware of His leading, and as well that he does hold your mistakes over your head as others may do. I'm eternally grateful that God's love has never failed me. I was so gullible and naive. As I matured, I began to become more aware and careful. This was one of several major lessons learned. Things could have turned out differently, nonetheless, the principle of letting go is key to healing so I could embrace my next. For many years I beat myself up over this incident, it even impacted me with my own

41

daughters. I always told them to meet the person at the place of the date and never let them bring you home. They probably thought this was strange Mom, but they didn't know of this incident in my life, but they followed my motherly advice.

Then one day Holy Spirit said you are forgiven. God has had to say this to me many times. I struggled with perfectionism. Knowing that my life had taken many bumps in the road caused me to look down on myself. My self-worth and self-esteem suffered because of this, and I found myself dealing with depression. This was the start of the cycle that I found myself in. I know what depression looks and feels like and I'm grateful to God for bringing me out. He is the lifter of my head and the lover of my soul. The inner turmoil was taking a toll on my life, my health and now my mind.

How did I get here? Life has a way of happening for us all. Through this, I learned even more that God is faithful and that He's mindful of me. Even this He could use for His glory. Nothing in life takes God by surprise and He reminded me continuously through His word that He loved me. I stand

encouraged today in the knowing that God can use any one and all of my life lessons. Those things that happened to me do not define who I am. I live in this truth now, that is the totality of who I was. It was a part of my past. Recognizing that I am a different person today one that has been through many things, but I made it out. Life happened! I lived and I learned. I have always been the one to try and learn from my mistakes but to not allow them to keep me in a place of what was, but rather embrace the here and now. The important thing I have learned is that for surety life will throw us some curve balls. I say throw it back and keep moving... Forward. If you have dealt with anything similar or an incident that has made you feel as if you did something to cause it, it's a lie and you can heal from it says God. I will meet you at your point of need. I can remove the shame and the pain of it all. There is a new horizon coming to you and it's here now. Will you accept all that God has for you? I say yes! I want the perfect plan of God for my life.

PRAYER

Father, today I thank you for healing of emotional hurt and the trauma of past events in my life. I no longer carry a victim mindset, but a survivor, an overcomer. Today I want to be "made whole." No longer will I live in the memory of it, the shame, or the humiliation. No longer fragmented. The Lord put the pieces back together again and make all things beautiful in your timing. I thank you that I am no longer bound by guilt and fear. I walk in liberty. I walk in the strength of God with peace, clarity and a sound mind. My heart is open to receiving your love and the love of others that you place in my path. Show me the way and lead me to those that you have predestined for me to meet. I thank you for the forward movement into the New, the Next and the Now. I thank you for every defining moment that helped shape me to be who you have called me to be. In Jesus's name, Amen.

03

LIFE LESSONS

LET'S DO THE WORK!

If you are dealing with childhood trauma or of any sort now would be the time to consult with a clinical professional for therapy or counseling.

For self-help: write a letter regarding your feelings in your journal.

This is a way of expressing your feelings and helps with letting things go.

Where no counsel is, the people fall: but in the multitude of counsellors there is safety. Proverbs 11:14 KJV

MANTLE MATCH

I WILL NO LONGER
LIVE IN WHAT WAS -
THE NEW IS UPON ME.

04
OVERCOMING REJECTION & DISTRACTION

As a young child, I was often given lots of responsibility. I was depended upon by my family, and I never wanted to let them down yet the spirit of rejection and not feeling loved kept me in cycles still. I don't know where this seed derived from but at an incredibly young age, I felt unloved and that I was not enough, there was this particular Thursday night at church. I was around the age of fifteen years old; that I had my first encounter with God. A minister by the name of Carol McDougal came to me and hugged me and said, "Yes you are loved," she also said, "Jesus loves you" and from then to now, I have always known that God was and is real. These simple yet profound words were just what I needed to hear. I had not shared what I was feeling with anyone but God in my prayers however, that seed would not die so quickly.

During my adolescent years and even into adulthood, I fought with this thing called rejection. Not even knowing it then, that was my struggle. Fast forward years later I found myself in relationships that were broken and loveless. The seed of rejection and loneliness were still there but I had yet to identify it. It wasn't until my failed marriage of eighteen years that The Lord said to me, "I'm breaking cycles off of your life and I'm going to heal you." The day I was in my Pastor's office, post-divorce, as we were discussing things, he said to me "You Are Enough" and these three words changed my life forever. With tears in my eyes, I knew that I would have to rely on God to heal me and release me from the pain.

I left Pastor's office knowing that I was enough and that I too, yes me deserved to be loved and you as well! Sometimes it's good to tell yourself that I too deserve it! This was invigorating to me! I value people and relationships. That's why it's important to let God reveal it, so He can heal it. Whatever your "IT" is, it's time to overcome it all. I'm reminded of *Jeremiah 30:17* *"For I will restore health unto thee, and I will heal thee*

of thy wounds, saith The Lord; because they called thee an Outcast, saying, This is Zion, whom no man seeketh after."

Even in my Christian walk, I had to deal with rejection in the church, within different organizations and I could not understand why I was dealing with this. So, not only was I feeling rejected in my personal life but also in my spiritual life. God has been revealing to me while on this **Mantle Match** journey, that even if you are rejected so you think by "man" I have not rejected you and you are loved. I now know this is and was a delusion to keep me off focus. This scripture comes to mind. *"Set your affection on things above, not on things on the earth." **Colossians 3:2*** This is what I started doing. I started recalling the word of God and what God had said about me and what was spoken over my life. Rejection is real and a hurtful thing, but we cannot live in this place. I was intentional about uprooting what was planted through prayer and worship before God. It was in His word that deliverance was taking place. NO longer in the shadow of my pain, I continued to allow God to make a beautiful piece of work out of my so-called broken life. He was doing work within me, and all of this was coming to the surface, and I was going through my journey. We often want the greater, the more and the increase but it comes with a price. A price that is worth it, if I must add. Never again will I devalue myself and neither should you.

I want to declare that you are enough! You are fearfully and wonderfully made by God. He says you are worthy, and He loves you. You Are Enough! God says this because you and I were created in His image to bring Him glory.

*"Not that we are sufficient of ourselves to think anything as of ourselves; but our sufficiency is of God." **2 Corinthians 3:5 NIV***

Principle four; Be healed! Your King/Queen is on the way, and we must love from a place of wholeness. No longer will we pour from a half-full glass. Will thou be made whole? I had made up my mind that from here on out I would be me and not allow what others thought of me to control my reflection of myself and how God saw me. This was liberating to me! I am known by name by God, and I have come to know him in a way that I have never known him before. I needed God to make

me free from the injuries of my life. I can remember praying to remove the memories of the pain and hurt. I didn't even want to remember all that I had dealt with, and God did honor some of that. There are things that I just can't remember today and I'm grateful that The Lord washed me in His word. *"That he might sanctify her, having cleansed her by the washing of water with the word." Ephesians 5:26*

Distractions come in countless shapes and forms. Oftentimes you are not aware that a distraction is one until you are too far into it. I found myself so distracted and off course, which kept me derailed. I thought that after I gave God my yes, my ministry would start, things would go smoothly, and all things would work out well. There was so much for me to learn. My "yes" required me to keep declaring my acceptance to surrender my life to The Lord repeatedly. The distractions were subtle and were exactly what I wanted. They were the "perfect mistakes". This is what I called them, and they were enough to keep me engaged and distracted from God's plan. I knew these distractions were of no benefit to me. That's when I recognized that I was in cycles yet again.

I begin to earnestly pray asking God to break the cycles and the ties that entangled me. I knew that I had to move past this, but it was so hard. This required much fasting and much prayer. My prayers changed, they had to. I needed guidance and direction from God to overcome rejections and distractions. NO MORE derailment! I became determined that I shall become who God has predestined me to be and it was time for me to go with God so that I could experience a breakthrough in my life. This was bigger than me! I gave God a yes for my children and for every generation that would come after me.

Zechariah 4:6 *"Then he answered and spake unto me, saying, This is the word of The LORD unto Zerubbabel, saying, Not by might, nor by power, but by my spirit, saith The LORD of hosts."*

As a people pleaser, trying to appease everyone had become daunting and draining. While seeking the approval and validation of man this caused me to lose focus. My desire to please The Lord was diminishing. I believe self-growth and development are necessary to improve and be the best version of yourself, but this should be done with a pure motive in my opinion this is what growth and maturity looks like.

By identifying this, I began to step into my uniqueness and embrace it fully. "Uniquely Me", which gives me the freedom to live my life out loud without any comparison. This allowed my authenticity to flourish and for me to be comfortable with who God had called me to be. Hiding behind a mask and not being yourself is another form of distraction and derailment that can keep you in this place of never measuring up and you do! Again, you are enough. The derailment of my true self-identity delayed the process and preparation that God was taking me through on this journey. Not knowing then what I know now, I felt as if I had wasted time and that I had messed up so much.

Remember I am and was still finding my way. So what I am not perfect, but I am chosen. That's what God said to me one day. "I still choose you, yes you!" I just love how God reminded me again of His love for me. His love never fails. He knows just what we need and when we need it. He is a loving father and I want to remind you that you are loved and that you are not a castaway!

All that the Father giveth me shall come to me; and him that cometh to me I will in no wise cast out. **John 6:37**

04

OVERCOMING REJECTION & DISTRACTIONS

LET'S DO THE WORK!

Find value in self...... give yourself self-care.
An example, Buy yourself fresh flowers.
Don't forget to document the journey in your journal. How did it make you feel? How did they smell?

Set your mind and keep focused habitually on the things above [the heavenly things], not on things that are on the earth [which have only temporal value].
Colossians 3:2 AMP

MANTLE MATCH

WITH EACH NEW DAY -
I AM GROWING AND
EVOLVING.

I am enough

MANTLE MATCH

05
I AM NOT PERFECT

Trusting God was not easy for me. In fact, it was hard; especially when I did not have all the details. That's when I had to move in faith. Faith is not knowing every detail before moving in what God has spoken, but rather moving in faith and trusting God to give the details when needed. I have a similar quote over my bed. I don't know how many times a day I read this as a gentle reminder to keep trusting in God. This is faith, acting on what God has spoken. Just like Abraham. God gave him a word to go, get from your kindred and your country and go to a land I will show you (emphasized). Faith moves God!

Just like Abraham, this next move would require faith. As I was riding in the car one day. God showed me a chess game and as I was studying the board God said to me this next move is on me. This was profound to me because I was seeking God about what was next. I was leaning into him for directions and clarity, and He spoke again. Facing the fact that I messed up too and a lot of situations I put myself in. I gave too much too soon and exposed myself to things that I should have never engaged in. This invited familiar spirits and strongholds into my life that would require God to tear down and dismantle. I needed God to help me, and He was ready to help me in my time of trouble. Principle five Forgiveness. This could be self-forgiveness or forgiveness of others. It must be addressed and dealt with.

Jesus gives us an illustration in *Matthew 18:23-25* that emphasizes the necessity of being forgiven and for extending forgiveness towards others. This is the parable about two debtors. What we expect of others, we should extend to others; with the measure you use, it will be measured to you. I could tell you of the countless times I felt that it wasn't my fault and asked why I should be the one to apologize or turn the other cheek? I had some spiritual maturing that was needed. But I learned that forgiveness is not a process it's a choice and that healing is a process, so then I chose to forgive because it was for me and not the other person. I needed to forgive myself so that I could move forward. I felt as if I was stuck in a place of no movement, and this did not feel good. It was a hard task, but I was determined to see it through. Healing is my portion. I didn't want to be stuck. Recently in a Sunday Bible lesson, we would discuss this very same principle. "The refusal to forgive others is an unpardonable sin" is what the lesson taught me.

I was so disappointed with the poor choices that I had made that I became ashamed and withdrawn. This was a tactic of the devil to keep me bound. I heard a sermon regarding "The Woman at the Well". This was a message of cycles and that for years she kept going through the same thing but that day she met a man named Jesus at the well that told her all she knew about herself, and she changed the lives of many because he offered her forgiveness. God changed her story! I was like this woman in many ways. I was this woman that had everything or so it seemed, yet I was broken and in need of healing. "I am not perfect" but God still loved me, and I could not understand why. I had an 'at the well' experience that changed my life forever. I was so wrapped up in the thoughts in my head that I had done so many things that I surely God didn't love me, nor could he use me for His glory. This was all an illusion that he was trying to keep me in. I was reassured of God's love repeatedly as I heard Him speak to me. God was doing a work within me. Healing was taking place, yet I could still hear the whispers in my ear; "you are not loved. How could God use you? God will never forgive you for all of that".

Then I started to embrace the Grace Factor. I had to call to silence all the negative thoughts and remind myself of the words that were spoken over of my life. Although I was not perfect, I was still chosen and selected by God. Go share what I have done for you and impact and inspire those whose paths you come by. We all have things that God wants us to do to advance the kingdom that will bring His name honor and glory.

*"Before I formed you in the womb, I knew you before you were born, I set you apart I appointed you as a prophet to the nations." **Jeremiah 1:5 NIV***

God can use it all and nothing that I had gone through canceled the assignment or change the mind of GOD concerning His plans for my life. He says, "I have called you by name and I called you unto myself and yes even that, I can use for my glory. I forgive you! You are LOVED"! At no time can we rely on our own strength; if we do, we will fail. We must trust God and His leading. He will not lead us astray. The victory has already been determined and the battle is declared. We are victorious. I didn't know who I was in God. I was not yet aware of my kingdom assignment and the plans of God for my life were not yet revealed, but NOW I know! This was mind blowing to me that yes me that God still use me and that he loved me. The love of a father is pretty amazing. My faith was increasing, and I could see God for who He really is. A loving, caring and compassion God. One that is slow to anger and forgiving. He stands with outstretched arms and He invites us into fellowship with him, into covenant relationship.

I want to add, you don't have to be perfect just willing and obedient the Bible says. Then we shall see the goodness of The Lord. The benefits of receiving His love outweigh any imperfections we may have. So, He said to me, *"This is the word of The Lord to Zerubbabel: 'Not by might nor by power, but by my Spirit, says The Lord Almighty. **Zechariah 4:6*** In God, with God, and by God.

05

I AM NOT PERFECT

LET'S DO THE WORK!

Create a treasure chest of affirmations that you can revisit at a later time and when needed. (write them in your journal and also get a jar/canister of some sort to put them in. Be creative!

Activity: Weekly select an affirmation from the treasure box and reflect and write in your journal whatever you are feeling or gathering from your affirmation.

And wisdom and knowledge shall be the stability of thy times, and strength of salvation: the fear of the LORD is his treasure. Isaiah 33:6

MANTLE MATCH

NO LONGER
FRAGMENTED,
THE MASTERS
HANDIWORK.
I AM WHOLE!

MANTLE
MATCH

06
YOU ARE ENOUGH

I was given a command to proclaim by way of Holy Spirit that *"You are Enough."* To know this, I needed to be made whole. Being whole means that your spirit, soul, and body are all aligned, healthy, and positioned towards The Lord. According to the Oxford Dictionary, being whole is the total amount or extent of; every part of, all; entire, full. Modifying a singular noun, following a determiner or possessive. Why is this important because it positioned me to know and accept that I am valuable to God and that I had everything that I needed to fulfill my kingdom assignment. During the First Morning Glory Summit, The Lord instructed me to bring the women together and speak to them that it was time to arise.

He took me to John 5:6, when Jesus saw him lie, and knew that he had been now a long time in that case, he saith unto him, Wilt thou be made whole? I ask the same question to you and

I. Wilt thou be made whole? The lame man begins to give excuses. I have no one to put me in when the water is troubled. Another comes before me and steps in front of me. Jesus said to him take up thy bed and walk. The thing that once carried him, he now carries. No longer will I be bound by this is or that thing. Will you take up your bed and walk, which is symbolic to moving forward? Putting those things behind us and pressing towards the mark of the high calling in Christ Jesus!

In *Luke 8:46* this passage of scripture tells the story of the widow who had been sick for twelve years with an issue of blood. You could say she was healed by accident. Why because Jesus was not looking or expecting to heal her. As a matter of fact, he was on his way to Jarius' house to heal his daughter. In this text, God asked another question; who touched me, for I perceive that virtue is gone out of me? God knew who she was!! Just like He knows who you and I are. God wanted her to identify herself so that she would know it wasn't in the garment but by her faith. You and I can touch him by

our faith. I have faith that I am enough It's our faith that pleases God.

Do you dare to believe that all that life has dealt you that God says I know who you are? I have called you by name. There's a plan for each of your lives and this day God says you are enough. I have called you into myself! I know what I have placed inside of you, for my glory. You are the salt of the earth.

God comes to destroy the works of darkness! We break the back of childhood trauma, the pain of past abuse and the secret sins. Wilt thou be made whole? Not in our own sufficient but in that of The Lord... I touched him through prayer by faith and He knows me because He created me before I was in my mother's wombs. Everything about you and I show forth His glory... it speaks to His splendor and majesty. God says His Grace is sufficient! This means this grace is enough so then you are enough.

No, it's not too late. You still have time to take up your bed and walk, no longer will you allow what happened to you and against you to stay down and in bondage! I choose to come up out of it. The angels are here, and the water is troubled.

You don't need anyone to put you in today God says I see you! Touch me with your faith! Your faith will make you whole! *"Now unto him who is able to do exceedingly and abundantly above what we ask or think, according to the power that works in you." **Ephesians 3:20*** That place of pain is where you will find purpose and the mess is your message share the love of God with others that will help them as well to pick up their bed and walk. What the devil meant for evil God will turn and use that too. It's working for your good!

It's time to push! Pray until something happens. Use whatever it was that you have endured and survived through and minister to others in the same situation, use the rape or molestation to help others be safe. That's how you pick up your bed and walk. Walk with it, through it and walk it out. According to **Ephesians 4:7**, you are graced for what you are carrying. Call! Chosen and Favored!! The levees are broken! No more restrictions! You are unstoppable!

YOU ARE ENOUGH! God says so. There are treasures inside of you.

You are one of a kind, a designer's original. I have deposited greatness within you, and I say that you are enough. I know you by name and I call you unto myself. I have forgiven your mistakes; you no longer live in what you were but now you embrace the New. I have equipped you with all that you need to complete your assignment. Your gifts, your abilities, and your talents all give me glory. You are enough because I say that you are. I shall have a return on my investment and what I have seeded within you.

I AM ENOUGH & SOMETHING GREAT IS COMING OUT OF ME!

Isaiah 45:3-5 NIV "I will give you hidden treasures, riches stored in secret places, so that you may know that I am The LORD, the God of Israel, who summons you by name. For the sake of Jacob my servant, of Israel my chosen, I summon you by name and bestow on you a title of honor, though you do not acknowledge me. I am The LORD, and there is no other; apart from me there is no God. I will strengthen you, though you have not acknowledged me."

06

YOU ARE ENOUGH!

LET'S DO THE WORK!

Seek the Lord for his purpose for your life and add a journal entry.

Knowing your purpose will keep you from going in cycles. We are moving in purpose!

Many are the plans in a person's heart, but it is the Lord's purpose that prevails. Proverbs 19:21

MANTLE MATCH

IN MY PLACE OF WAIT –
I FAST, PRAY&
WORSHIP. IT WILL BE
WORTH THE WAIT!

MANTLE
MATCH

07
THE WAIT

The mantle represented a man's gift, the call of God, and the purpose for which God had called him. The mantle served as a symbolic purpose, in the case of the prophets, showing they were wrapped in God's authority. It is also a position of authority or responsibility. There is a responsibility as we are waiting. God is requiring us to participate in this season. We must be in a state of producing. God spoke to me one day and said, "He will find you when you are in your purpose." God has been speaking to me to worship, pray, and wait. How befitting that is since it sounds like Hannah's story. She wanted a child, a male child to be specific, and she prayed earnestly for one. Commentary suggests it had been twenty years and Hannah still had not conceived. We know the part of the story where she gave her husband consent to take another wife Peninnah because she was barren. After one visit to Shiloh, Hannah cried out to God and

the Priest Eli came in agreement with her and God remembered Hannah, but that's not how the story ended.

Hannah vowed to God that she would give him to God for all the days of his life if He blessed her with a man child and when it happened, she kept her promise. *1 Samuel 2:20-21* Hannah's vow to God gives us a glimpse into her love for God and how she honored God. Hannah never asked God for more children, but God blessed her because of her willingness. God gave her more than she expected, and just like Hannah, it's going to be worth the wait. Each of our stories will be different and the timing in which the promise manifests itself, but the Bible also records that while Hannah prayed to God, she worshipped and then she produced. She participated, she partnered with God and the promise manifested. Hannah had to wait on the appointed time and the same holds true for you and I. Principle six **Wait on God**. What will you be found doing in the wait?

The wait can be a difficult time, or it could be the best time. It's all about how I choose to look at it, So I made the most and best of it. There were things that Hannah did in the process. She fasted, she prayed, she worshiped and then produced. Wow, there was an exchange. Hannah forgot what she didn't have and instead, she set her focus on God and then the promise manifested itself right before her very eyes. In God's timing, it came to pass. The Lord remembered her, as well he will remember you also. You are not forgotten. The Bible records in *1 Samuel 1:17* that the prophet came in agreement with Hannah. *"Then Eli answered and said, Go in peace: and the God of Israel grant thee thy petition that thou hast asked of him."* The power of agreement. It was only after Hannah and her husband arose early the morning after the encounter with the prophet that Hannah produced.

I come in agreement with you today that God would grant you your very heart's desires as they align to His will. Alignment with God and His will is a must so that we are not going in our way and strength. He wants us to depend on Him and Him alone. Hannah also came in alignment with God's plans for Samuel her son's life that God gave her the thing that she had been praying for. *"When the time is right, I The Lord will make it happen." Isaiah 60:22 NLT*

When I began to set my affections on things above and not on this world then I felt a settling from within and I knew that God had me right where He wanted me, and I was enjoying my time with God. In His presence is the fullness of joy. The wait was necessary. Whew! Yes, it was necessary for me. This was a much-needed time for me. I was provoked to produce. God had spoken, "He will find you when you are in your place of promise." I am following Holy Spirit as He leads. I became even more intentional about my kingdom assignment, not because I wanted a significant other but because I wanted GOD! My perspective has shifted and now I see what God is doing in my life.

He was bringing me to an awareness of the mantle, the mandate and the mission that was on my life. I had work to do, and it was time to get to it. In the wait, I was releasing all that was holding me back from walking into what God had for me. Then he began to speak to me concerning my potential &

destiny. He asked me a question, "Are you willing to be a change agent"? An individual who instigates or implements change within a social unit or situation (e.g., a family or group) or an organization by communicating to, managing, and encouraging others in the change. My answer was yes Lord, again I was surrendering my will. I prayed for this, and I am welcoming it. I want to be the change that people need and see. In the wait I work, I create, and I do. He has already promised me that he's gone before me to make crooked places straight and to tear down any oppositions that try to block the work of that my hands are required to.

For many, it may have been a long time, for others a short while, in any instance you don't need a significant other to start any projects or endeavors. Just work as unto The Lord. Eli Roi the God that sees me. This has been a common thread in Mantle Match that God says he sees.

That is magnificent to know that he sees us not only that, but he hears, and he cares. I am no longer invisible. I am His and he is mine. His love for me has always been and always will be.

The oneness with the Father has healed me. In the wait I stay in faith; I stay in His presence and there I will have everything that I need this keeps me grounded and focused on the main thing and that is my relationship with God. God is not going to allow anything or anyone that will take you or I away from him. In my times of prayer, I vowed to God that I would always put him first in my life and I mean that. I plan to keep the main thing the main thing even when he finds me. God is my number one priority.

AFFIRMATION: IN THE WAIT I WORSHIP!

Ecclesiastes 4:9-12 NIV "Two are better than one, because they have a good return for their labor: If either of them falls down, one can help the other up. But pity anyone who falls and has no one to help them up. Also, if two lie down together, they will keep warm. But how can one keep warm alone? Though one may be overpowered, two can defend themselves. A cord of three strands is not quickly broken."

MAKE ALL THINGS BEAUTIFUL AGAIN IN TIME

Ecclesiastes 3

To everything there is a season, and a time to every purpose under the heaven:

A time to be born, and a time to die; a time to plant, and a time to pluck up that which is planted.

A time to kill, and a time to heal; a time to break down, and a time to build up.

A time to weep, and a time to laugh; a time to mourn, and a time to dance.

A time to cast away stones, and a time to gather stones together; a time to embrace, and a time to refrain from embracing.

A time to get, and a time to lose; a time to keep, and a time to cast away.

A time to rend, and a time to sew; a time to keep silence, and a time to speak.

A time to love, and a time to hate: a time of war, and a time of peace.

What profit hath he that worketh in that wherein he laboureth?

I have seen the travail, which God hath given to the sons of men to be exercised in it.

He hath made everything beautiful in His time: also, he hath set the world in their heart, so that no man can find out the work that God maketh from the beginning to the end.

PRAYER

Father, I take solace in your word according to this passage of scripture that you will make all things beautiful in your timing. Although I don't fully understand every detail of my life, I know there's a purpose and nothing will be wasted. Through all these things, I will see the good out of my current situation. Your ways are not my ways, and your thoughts are higher than mine. Give me strength where needed and endurance to keep looking to you. As I "go and do" new endeavors give me direction and clarity. This wait is preparing me for the manifestation of the promise that is to come. I come into agreement with those who are waiting. Just as the prophet Eli said to Hannah, "Go in peace: and the God of Israel grant thee thy petition that thou hast asked of him." Lord any day now, however, your timing is the best time. Thank you for this day and time of oneness with you. Amen.

07

THE WAIT

LET'S DO THE WORK!

- Find a new café, or restaurant and treat yourself to a brunch, or dinner. Take yourself on a date.

- Journal the journey so that you can always reflect on this time with you and God alone.

I will praise thee; for I am fearfully and wonderfully made: marvellous are thy works; and that my soul knoweth right well. Psalm 139:14 KJV

MANTLE MATCH ™

I AM " UNIQUELY ME" –
PURPOSED WITH
POTENTIAL.

MANTLE
MATCH

08
I AM WHOLE

Not knowing then what I know today is that everything I had gone through was for a purpose and every defining moment would bring glory to God and give Him praise. As a woman in ministry, along with all other roles and responsibilities, I carried, I never saw this. I just thought life was hard and unfair. As my spiritual eyes began to open more and more my focus shifted.

A diadem is a headband or crown worn especially as a symbol of royalty. One definition of royalty is a right of jurisdiction granted to an individual or corporation by a sovereign. The Sovereign God had spoken, again I was God's chosen. I kept hearing in my spirit you are a "diadem in my hands." God was saying to me you will bring me glory, your life will testify of my goodness. This blessed me tremendously given the lack of confidence that I had in myself for what God was asking of me to do.

*"Thou shall also be a crown of glory in the hand of The Lord, and a royal diadem in the hand of God." **Isaiah 62:3***

To hear these words, begin to solidify the love of my father for me unconditionally. Life had knocked the breath out of me, but I kept getting up and I kept moving forward. Perseverance and Resilience is what these times required of me. I almost flatlined but God resuscitated me. The fresh breath of God caused Purpose to be awakened from within. I could no longer live in the past of what was, it was now time to embrace the new and the now.

Each of us has an assignment in the earth and I had not yet fully grasped mine, nor the magnitude of what God was calling for me to, but now I get it. Each day brought a renewed joy from within. I had decided to do it God's way. At one time, I had obligations that had me pressed for time and every day I would put on my GPS (Global Positioning System) to obtain the quickest route home, but I would never follow the route given,

why? Because I was so accustomed to doing it my way and going the familiar way route home. Until one day I arrived home late. I don't like to be late, and this was important to me. I had a prior commitment that I needed to keep.

During this time, I prayed to The Lord to help me to get home by the necessary time so that I could keep my obligations. Holy Spirit spoke so clearly to me, "I have been trying to take you another way", I said this a few chapters ago. God began saying to me "A way less traveled and you will arrive home safely and on time". I was missing God by not following His leading. I only needed to submit to doing it God's way, which was the best way and not that of my own. Not doing so brought on stress, delays, and frustration. This is important because in this timing is it going to require obedience to God. This is the season to obey God. All His commands, not just the ones I liked. Ouch, Lord. That hurt! Once I came into alignment with God and His will, I began to see the hand of God move. My obedience released the blessings and favor from God. I want all that God has for me. I was intentional about obeying God.

"If ye be willing and obedient, ye shall eat the good of the land."
Isaiah 1:19

God used this situation to speak to me again to confirm that He is in control of my life and my destiny. In this, I reflected on how many times had I gone my own way and missed God. That's why it is important to be in sync with Holy Spirit. All I had to do was allow him to lead the way.

AFFIRMATION:
I WILL OBEY GOD! I AM WHOLE IN PURPOSE

"For she said, If I may touch but his clothes, I shall be whole."
Mark 5:28

The woman with the issue of blood needed healing just as I did. Her healing was physical and mine also, but I also needed emotional healing as well. It was twelve years she had suffered and gone to many physicians. Spending all that she had and still she was not better. I can relate to this because it took me years. More than thirteen years to see that I too needed to "Be Made Whole" which was principle seven.

My journey was not easy but for everything I endured it was necessary for my growth and development. It shaped me to be who God has called me to be. *"He said unto her, Daughter, be of good comfort: thy faith hath made thee whole; go in peace".* **Luke 8:48** Today I say to myself and you. Go in peace and be made whole! Now Faith is perceiving that what God had spoken over my life would manifest. I decree it's coming to pass. At first, when I started hearing from God regarding Mantle Match, I thought it would be a book of principles given to me on what to do while I waited on God to send my husband what I thought was (The Mantle Match) but about two principles in, I knew this was no longer the focus. What was really on the mind of God was about getting me to a place of wholeness to embrace the mantle that was on my life and the mandate so that the real Mantle is Matched. See, at a very young age I knew I was different, called, and unique, but it wasn't until I was much older that I no longer saw this as a flaw but rather as a blessing. Once I began to embrace the call on my life that's when my kingdom assignment became clear.

I don't need a significant other to be whole. I am complete in God. I'm already loved, I am already chosen, I know who I am and whose I am.

The great God that I serve was preparing, processing me, bringing healing, and self-forgiveness so that I would Match (pair & accept) the Mantle that he had already predestined for me before I was formed in my mother's womb. While I was waiting, I discovered that life happens, I'm not perfect and many lessons were learned, both good and bad ones; and that it's okay. I now know my purpose. This was a blessing to me! My God. I know who I am, and I accept what He says about me. I'm a conduit for Christ. I am matched with my Mantle because I agree with God. I align with His will and His plans for me.

In my waiting, I am whole. I am complete and every day I am working on me. There's a continual seeking for God not a spouse. It never was. I know that when the time is right, he will find me in and on purpose just as God said. I trust the timing of God, knowing it's going to be worth the wait. The wait!!! The wait!!! The wait!!! I will honor God in my wait. I hear Daniel 1:8. I will stay in faith and keep looking into him who is the author and the finisher of my faith. I am whole.

My dear friend Joey said to me, "You are not a broken woman. You are one of the most complete and whole women that I know. He also said, "You don't need a man to complete you, you already are". God will send you confirmation when needed. He didn't know I was writing this chapter, but God did! God began using this man to speak into my life, it was almost as if God let him eavesdrop on our conversations and prayers. This was yet another defining moment for me. "I have healed you," says God! So today I am reinforced by God so that I can bring encouragement to His people. My mission is to Build, Impact and Inspire. As well as remind God's people that they are loved and that he still saves. So simple but profound.

Love is a powerful attribute that we share not only with God but with each other. Knowing this I did not want to do what I had seen done before: to minister from a place of hurt and then turn that pain on God's people. That's one of the reasons why I did not want to step into the mandate given to me by God. On the other hand, I thought that if I did this pain would go away but oh was I so wrong. It was not until I allowed God to bring all of it to the surface that I was truly able to be delivered. It was almost like I was in a dressing room, discarding those things that I didn't like and the things that did not serve me purpose. There was much turmoil within as I was and still am being processed. I heard a preacher say, "that God will often time hide as he processes you then he will present you. My process was needed to bring me to a place of wholeness. I am recalling a dream I had in late 2022 where The Lord showed me in my dream a spool of fabric. It was so beautiful with shades of green and gold (He knows I love the color green) in it and there was a chair that the fabric was lying next to, and I thought there was no way this was enough to cover this chair. This is what I was thinking as my dream was unfolding itself. I thought it was there to cover the chair, then The Lord said to me I am changing your garments.

The Significance of Changing Garments is very powerful as it represents that you are moving from glory to glory and exchanging the "old" for the "new". God says I'm doing a new thing in your life and yes there was and still is an exchange. I chose to lay aside the old me. The baggage and the weight of it all for what God wants to do in my life. God wanted to do the new thing in me, and I was now willing to allow him to do that. Not understanding what that would look like. I gave God another yes. My yes to God carried weight in the realm of the spirit.

Then Jesus gave them this illustration: *"No one tears a piece of cloth from a new garment and uses it to patch an old garment. For then the new garment would be ruined, and the new patch wouldn't even match the old garment. "And no one puts new wine into old wineskins. For the new wine would burst the wineskins, spilling the wine, and ruining the skins. New wine must be stored in new wineskins. But no one who drinks the old wine seems to want the new wine. 'The old is just fine,' they say.* **Luke 5:36-39 NLT.** There has been a release and an exchange.

Another defining moment in my life was embracing the call. No longer will I counsel with man regarding what God has spoken over my life. I will no longer walk in shame with my head down because of what I have gone through and endured, even the testing. God can use it all to bring His name glory. It was not all just for me, but for those that would cross my path. I can share my story and testimony that shows the goodness and mercy of God. I move forward with the knowledge and reassurance from God that all things will work together for the good, to those who love God, to those who are the called according to His purpose. *Romans 8:28*

I have a new outlook on life and with forward movement, I keep pressing. Just as God had spoken, he will find me in purpose. I am still in my wait and while I wait on the special someone God has for me, I will keep these principles and those in the word of The Lord near to me. I will put them into action. By staying in faith, I keep pressing. I know that God is not a man that he can lie. Our God is faithful. God has said to me before, take care of my business and I will take care of yours.

I will continue to do all that God is requiring my hands to do, trusting His plan, His will, and His timing! Nothing goes unnoticed by God. He is truly a Rewarder of those who diligently seek Him. Not just His hand but His face. The Mantle is Matched!

But seek first His kingdom and His righteousness, and all these things will be given to you as well. Matthew 6:33 NIV

A PROPHETIC WORD

Can I not do with you as the potter did with the clay? In my hand, I want to make you over again. Though the clay was marred, I can put the piece back together again, according to *Jeremiah 18:6*. You are my masterpiece. Crafted by me to bring me glory. I am the potter, and you are the clay. I have shaped you in my image. Your life reflects my glory. You are whom I say that you are, wonderfully made. You are mine. Daughter/son, I have always loved you and always will. Be healed, Be made whole. From the finished work of the cross I have already declared it. No more shame, of what happened that was beyond your control and even the things that were. There are no more regrets. For I will heal your wounds and restore your health. A crown of glory in my hand. I love you, yes you, says God. This place that you are in is not the end. I have a plan for your life. The things I have spoken, shown, and given you a glimpse of will come to pass.

*"Brethren, I count not myself to have apprehended: but this one thing I do, forgetting those things which are behind, and reaching forth unto those things which are before, I press toward the mark for the prize of the high calling of God in Christ Jesus." **Philippians 4:13-14***

AFFIRMATION: I AM WHOLE!

08

I AM WHOLE

LET'S DO THE WORK!

- Be intentional by being more mobile through physical exercise.
  *Examples: Jogging, Yoga, walking or whatever you are able to do. Just start!

- Today I am worthy to be loved. I love myself and I am loved by my creator. I will take care of my temple.

"Beloved, I pray that all may go well with you and that you may be in good health, as it goes well with your soul."

3 John 1:2

MANTLE MATCH

I AM YOUR HELPMEET
& YOUR LOVER- YOU
ARE SAFE IN MY ARMS.
MANTLE MATCH

09
DEAR FUTURE HUSBAND

It Is God's Decree!

Dear future husband, I have prayed for you! Thank you for loving me unconditionally. Thank you for the encouragement that you will give and for all the long talks we shall have. I can't wait to be in your arms to feel comforted and protected. I'm grateful that God created you just for me and me for you. Your kindness, your thoughtfulness and your love are unprecedented. I have been preparing and waiting patiently for you. I am honored that you have chosen me to walk with you as we push each other in our kingdom assignments. You are established and settled, my "God man."

You are a tailor-made man by God and a designer's original. God created me with you in mind. You are humble yet confident in the things of God and in life. You trust Him with your life, and you honor him. So, then I will honor you and follow you as you follow Christ. We will build together, travel to see the world and our lives will show forth the glory of God. God is so amazing. I'm truly blessed to have you.

Your Future Wife!

MANTLE MATCH

DEAR FUTURE HUSBAND

Preparedness... This time was for me to prepare myself mentally, physically, emotionally, and financially. I was making ready for use & consideration for both God and you. I wait with anticipation of when God will join us together. My priority in life is to please God and to serve Him with my whole heart. God says, today I am molding you. So, I remain pliable in His hands. Willing and obedient. Together we can continue to prepare for the next that God endeavors us to. Together as one.

Until then...

Your Future Wife!

DEAR FUTURE HUSBAND

Process... I'm reminded of Esther. If I perish, I perish. But I'm going to see the King. This became my prayer. My stance was Lord, I trust you, no matter what and I look forward to the time that I can share with you intimately. I believe all that God did for me, will enhance your life as well. He that has begun a good work in me, shall complete it until the day of Jesus Christ. I say yes to the processing of The Lord so that I may walk worthy of the call and the vocation that is before me. How can two walk together expect they agree? Today my prayer for us is that we agree with God, with Heaven and with each other. The Power of Agreement.

Until Then...

Your Future Wife!

DEAR FUTURE HUSBAND

Life Lessons... Whew! I have learned and grown so much. Life is different today in a good way. I see through the lens of God now and not my own eyes. I acknowledge all the things I didn't do right, and I move forward. Life is about evolving and growing, and I have done that and will continue to grow. That's a part of life. I no longer beat myself up over what was, is or even what's to come. I rest in God's hand knowing that His word is true. And we know that all things work together for good to them that love God, to them who are the called according to his purpose. Hunny it was for His Purpose!

Until Then...

Your Future Wife!

DEAR FUTURE HUSBAND

Overcoming Rejection & Distractions.... And the victory has been won! The day The Lord whispered this in my ear, and I felt it in my spirit, I knew things had turned around for me. His love is like none other I have ever received. God is utterly amazing. I can trust Him at all times. When I needed Him the most He was there. I prayed and asked Him to silence all the noise so I could hear His voice and to uproot the seed of rejection from my life so that I would be open to loving you without restraints and He did that for me. I am excited for what He will do next. This journey was long but so worth it. Every day brings new insight and new wisdom. I am grateful for this time of evolution.

Until Then...

Your Future Wife!

MANTLE MATCH

DEAR
FUTURE HUSBAND

I am not perfect... that's my truth. I stand in that today knowing this. I'm not perfect but I am forgiven. That's what God said to me. So, I did a thing- I forgave myself also. I remove myself from the toxic thoughts and patterns of yesterday year. I walk in the confidence of God's love and His truth that He will make all things beautiful in time! I forgot those things that where behind me, and I press steadfastly forward. I embrace all that God has for us to share in our new. What was, is no longer and what is will be.

Until Then...

Your Future Wife!

DEAR FUTURE HUSBAND

You are enough... When The Lord gives you a word like this love, it's one you just have to sit with. He says I am enough. Not because of my beauty, my size, my intellect, or my abilities but because He knows what He has invested in me, and for what He has called me to do. I am fully equipped to do just that with no comparison. When I stand beside you with my arm in your arm, I will be confident in knowing who I am and whose I am. There is a certainty that comes from God that I am a chosen daughter, and you are who I say you are.

Until Then...

Your Future Wife!

DEAR FUTURE HUSBAND

The Wait... I love how God highlighted Hannah to me very early on! He knew that I would need this to help me remain faithful to the things of God and in this season to not lose hope. I learned the principles of fasting, praying, worshiping, and waiting! This time has been wonderful being in the presence of The Lord and hearing Him has given me strategic direction and clarity. In the wait, I came to know God like never before. The wait will be worth it. Not just for what He will give me with you but because of the exchange that took place between Him and I.

Until Then...

Your Future Wife!

DEAR FUTURE HUSBAND

I AM Whole... This Mantle Match journey has brought such a discovery of healing that was necessary. I asked God that before I met you that I would be freed from the baggage I carried for years from my past so that I could embrace your love without reservations. I wanted you to have God's best version of me. While I am still not perfect, I am being perfected through the love of Christ. I am no longer bitter, frustrated or confused about who I am. This is an intricate detail in process and my exploring the defining moments that make me who I am. I am prepared, processed, healed and whole as I wait on the promise.

Until Then...

Your Future Wife!

MANTLE MATCH

09
DEAR FUTURE SPOUSE

LET'S DO THE WORK!

↝

Write a series of letters to God about what you want in a spouse listing all of the kingdom attributes you desire.

Also write a letter to your future spouse as God leads you.

Then the Lord replied: "Write down the revelation and make it plain on tablets so that a herald may run with it.
Habakkuk 2:2

MANTLE MATCH

MY M ANTLE MATCH CHECKLIST

Month: .... **Week:** ....

Tasks	Su	Mo	Tu	We	Th	Fr	Sa
	✓						

APPENDIX

01/2/2023 Mantle of GOD - Kindle edition by Rosas, Carlos Luis. Religion ...

01/2/2023 https://dictionary.cambridge.org/us/dictionary/english/mantle

02/04/2023 Royalties Definition & Meaning - Merriam-Webster

04/15/2023 A Royal Diadem – Life and God

05/25/2023 Diadem Definition & Meaning - Merriam-Webster

08/09/2023 The Significance of Changing Garments - God Encounters Ministries

01/15/2024 Match Definition & Meaning - Merriam-Webster

01/15/2024 APA Dictionary of Psychology

Prepare 01/25/2023 prepare verb - Definition, pictures, pronunciation and usage notes | Oxford Advanced American Dictionary at OxfordLearnersDictionaries.com

12/26/2023 What Is a Process? | Business Transformation | FLOvate (micology.com)

01/04/2024 One accord winter 2023-2024 Adult student guide by Pathway Press

HEY THERE, I'M KISHA

Kisha R. Purnell is a native of South Carolina. Called at a young age, she began singing when she was just four years old. She had an earnest love for God. God anointed and chose her according to Jeremiah 1:5. "Before I formed you in the womb. I knew you before you were born. I set you apart; I appointed you as a prophet to the nations. She currently resides in North Carolina with her two daughters' Kaylyn and Jakyia. Kisha's gift as a 'Prophetic Intercessor' to God's people was birthed through intercession and worship. She is passionate about inspiring God's people through songs that provoke worship and sharing God's word. She attributes her love for God to her grandmother and mother's teachings and their training her up in the way of the Lord. Kisha is recognized by many as a servant leader of Christ and is humble to serve God and His people. She is the founder of K.R. Global Ministries. The goal of the ministry is to provide biblical principles that have a core focus on prayer and teaching the word of God to offer hope and restoration to the lives of God's people. Making it known that Jesus still saves and that He is the way. Kisha is God's vessel, for His people, for His glory!

Kisha

WELCOME TO THE

M

MANTLE MATCH JOURNEY

JOIN THE MANTLE MATCH ONLINE COMMUNITY!

MANTLE **M**ATCH ™

WWW.MANTLEMATCH.COM
@MANTLEMATCH

  clubhouse

www.ingramcontent.com/pod-product-compliance
Lightning Source LLC
Chambersburg PA
CBHW072126090426
42739CB00012B/3082